Reiki

A Beginner's Guide to
Energy Healing

Taylor Turner

Table of Contents

Introduction

Reiki is an often-misunderstood healing modality. Some people think it's "woo-woo" and argue that it makes no scientific sense. Others have witnessed and experienced its power and know in their bones that the energy is real and alive.

In this book, I will approach the evidence with an open mind, and present the facts and knowledge that I have found through my own research and experience. Together, we will determine what Reiki actually is and how it works. I'll take you through the history of Reiki so that you know where it came from and how ancient the technique is. We'll then go on a journey through the different levels of Reiki and cover all the potential benefits of this healing technique. Once we've gone that deep into the rabbit hole, you'll want to stay with me because then it gets really interesting!

I will then explain the training behind becoming a Reiki practitioner, the symbols and hand positions used (which are usually only revealed during training with a master), as well as how to perform Reiki from a distance and on animals. We'll even dip our toes into the idea that Reiki can be performed on multiple people at the same time and that healing energy can be sent around the globe.

There is something undeniable— we all have vital energy flowing through and around our bodies. This energy flows freely in some people, while in others, there are obvious blockages. Reiki opens up a way for healing to take place and for everyone to experience the thrill of true liberation. Once you have felt that universal light moving through you, there is no going back.

But let's start at the beginning, shall we?

Chapter 1: What is Reiki?

Reiki is a form of energy healing that is used primarily for stress reduction and relaxation. The technique originated in Japan during the early 20th century. The premise of this practice is that we all have an unseen life force energy that flows through our bodies. When we are stressed or unwell, this energy can be blocked in certain areas, and a Reiki practitioner moves their hands just above the client's body to restore the healthy flow of energy.

As energy is guided through the body, the client's self-healing abilities help to restore health and well-being. It's not the Reiki practitioner that has the healing powers, nor are they the source of the energy. The practitioner is simply there to channel the energy and restore the natural flow.

You can visualize what happens in a Reiki session by imagining what happens when blood is filtered through a dialysis machine. The "dirty" blood moves from the patient's body, through the machine that filters the blood, and then the "clean" blood re-enters the patient. In a Reiki session, the client's energy (which may be sticky or clogged) moves through the channel of a trained practitioner and then flows back through the client's body (now clear and unstuck).

The term "Reiki" is a combination of two Japanese words. The first is "rei," which means "God's wisdom'" or "spiritually guided." The second is "ki," which means "life force energy." This "ki" exists in all living things, including people, animals, and plants.

How Does Reiki Work?

There isn't sufficient scientific evidence to definitively answer how Reiki works. However, some theories make logical sense. One involves a phenomenon known as the "biofield." This is an electromagnetic field that exists within and around every living being. If you've ever experienced the shock of static electricity after creating friction with your body against another object, then you have felt this electromagnetic field.

The human heart has its own electrical field that can be measured with an electrocardiogram (ECG). This electricity is used to regulate our heartbeats. The brain and nervous system also contain multiple channels of electricity (this is how nerves send messages to each other). Every single cell in our body produces some level of electrical charge, which in turn create magnetic fields.

The idea that this electromagnetic field extends beyond our bodies makes sense. It is believed by some that this electric field extends more than 15 feet beyond our body.

This can also explain how the connection between two electromagnetic fields (practitioner and client) can cause a response.

The biofield is believed to guide bodily functions such as breathing and digestion. The change in energy flow during a Reiki session influences the body's electromagnetic field. When there are vibrational shifts in this biofield, it can potentially alter the physiological and psychological functioning in the client's body.

Another theory that may explain how Reiki works is quantum physics, a discipline that studies the interactions between energy and physical matter. Physicists have discovered that tiny particles of energy (such as electrons and photons) can exist in more than one place at the same time and that thoughts can influence how they behave. Considering this discovery, it isn't too far a stretch to consider that a Reiki practitioner can direct energy through the client by using their own thoughts and intentions.

10 Things That Weaken Life Force Energy

1. Excessive alcohol

2. Poor diet

3. Lack of exercise

4. Drugs

5. Smoking

6. Negative habits (such as self-harm)

7. Stress

8. Poor breathing

9. Lack of sleep and adequate rest

10. Negative psychic activity (such as negative thoughts)

The Seven Chakras

There are at least seven energy centers in our body. These hubs of energy are called chakras, which mean "wheels." It is believed that they are spinning disks of energy (some going clockwise and others counterclockwise) that need to remain open and aligned.

They each respond to specific bundles of nerves, organs, and areas of our energetic body (or life force energy).

Where Are They in the Body?

- The crown chakra is on top of the head and represents enlightenment, intuition, and spiritual vision. Energy from the crown chakra is directed to the pineal gland, upper brain, and right eye.

- The third eye chakra is found just above the eyebrows in the middle of the forehead. It connects to psychic perception, telepathy, and extrasensory perception (ESP). Energy from this chakra is transmitted to the central nervous system, spine, lower brain, left eye, pituitary gland, nose, and ears.

- The throat chakra is positioned in the middle of the neck and is associated with self-expression, emotional regulation, communication, and creativity. Energy from the throat chakra moves to the throat, thyroid gland, upper lungs, arms, and gastrointestinal tract.

- The heart chakra is found in the center of the chest, and it represents love, spiritual growth, devotion, and compassion. Energy flows from the heart chakra to the heart, circulatory system, thymus gland, liver, and lungs.

- The solar plexus chakra is positioned just above the navel. It's the center point of the body and is the area where digestion takes place and physical energy is generated to be sent throughout the body. Subtle energy moves from the solar plexus to the stomach, liver, digestive tract, gallbladder, and pancreas.

- The sacral chakra is found just below the navel. It corresponds to sexual energy, perceptions, and the first impressions of others. Energy is forwarded to the reproductive organs, legs, and glands.

- The root chakra is situated in the area of the genitals. It symbolizes life, physical vitality, birth, creativity, and security. Energy moves from the root chakra to the spine, kidneys, bladder, and adrenal glands.

Reiki and Chakras

During a Reiki treatment, the practitioner may work with these main centers of energy. Here are some specific ways that energy healing can open and align the chakras:

- The crown chakra is our connection to the universe and divine guidance. When Reiki energy is targeted at the crown chakra, it can lead to an immense sense of trust, safety, and oneness.

- The third eye chakra helps us see all that is not made of matter. It is our hub of intuition, clairvoyance, and psychic perception. If this chakra is blocked or misaligned, it can be difficult to trust our insights. Reiki healing can unblock this energy to reconnect us with our inner knowing.

- The throat chakra allows us to speak our truth. Imbalances here can manifest as thyroid issues or a sore throat. We may become wary of silence or fear judgment and rejection. Reiki clearing directed at the throat chakra helps us to express ourselves and find our voice again.

- The heart chakra connects to how we feel, our emotions, and how we express our love. A blocked heart chakra can make us feel lonely and disconnected from ourselves and others. Reiki targeting the heart chakra releases a flood of compassion and opens us up to receiving love.

- The solar plexus chakra is our power center. It's where we connect to our sense of self and our place of self-protection. If we feel scattered and direct all of our energy outwards, it can be a sign that we have given some of our power away and that our solar plexus chakra is imbalanced. Some people even feel discomfort or a whirling sensation in this area of the body, along with fatigue and possible cramping of the stomach. When blockages of this chakra are lifted through Reiki, it clears the way and empowers us to take targeted action.

- The sacral chakra is connected to sex, gender, creativity, and procreation. Sexual abuse or trauma often creates profound energy blockages in this chakra. Reiki can help lift these deeply suppressed emotions from that knot of restricted energy and release them (this is usually in the form of anger). The healing possibilities here are tremendous.

- The root chakra connects to our sense of identity, survival, and connection to the Earth. Fears around personal and financial security are usually linked to this chakra. Healing Reiki energy directed at this chakra gives us the sense that we are grounded and supported.

What Happens in a Reiki Session?

Reiki can be performed anywhere, even across vast distances. However, when the healing work is done in person, the fully-clothed client will sit on a comfortable chair or lie on a table. The room should be quiet and have a relaxing atmosphere. There may also be gentle music in the background if the client prefers.

The Reiki practitioner will lightly place their hands on, or slightly above, specific areas of the head, limbs, and torso. They'll use different hand shapes, depending on the specific area of the body or particular need. For example, if there is a particular injury, such as a sprained ankle, the hands will be held just above the troubled area.

As the practitioner hovers their hands over different parts of the body, there is a transfer of energy. They usually stay in one place for two to five minutes, and their hands often get warmer and start to tingle. The practitioner will hold the position of their hands until they sense the energy has stopped flowing in that particular area.

They'll pick up this depletion of energy when their hands no longer feel warm, if they lose the buzz or tingle, or sometimes only through intuition. Once this happens, they will move their hands over a different area of the client's body.

Different Reiki Techniques

Beaming

Beaming uses the distant healing symbol (this is usually visualized but can also be drawn with a finger on the palm). The practitioner then "beams" Reiki energy to a client across the room or even across the internet to a person on the other side of the world.

Beaming can treat the client's whole aura at once and then enter the body. Reiki energy can also be beamed directly to a specific area. It's much like using your hands as a magnifying glass reflecting the sun, focusing strong, healing light on the area you want to treat.

Beaming can be performed at the end of a standard treatment or by itself.

Smoothing and Raking the Aura

This is usually done before or after a healing treatment. The practitioner sweeps their hands through the client's aura or energy field. Aura smoothing or sweeping removes any superficial energy build-ups in the client's energy field. It brings a sense of harmony and balance, and it is a very calming practice.

Crystals and Chakra Healing Wands

Although a practitioner only needs their hands to perform a Reiki treatment, there are some crystals and stones that can help to restore the flow of energy. Some crystals are able to absorb negative energy, and all of them carry their own flow or "ki" that can be used to unblock particular areas of the body. Their unique vibration can align with the client's energy to assist with healing.

Now that you have a fair idea of what Reiki is and how it works, let's have a look at where it all started.

Chapter 2: The History of Reiki

Reiki, as it is practiced in the Western world today, was originally developed in the 1920s by a Buddhist priest, Mikao Usui (also known as Usui-Sensei). Although there were other styles of Reiki in Japan at the time, they were not as widely known, and Mikau Usui created his own style that we still use today: Usui Reiki.

Usui fasted and meditated for three weeks on Mount Kurama, which is a sacred mountain to the north of Kyoto, Japan. It was after this experience that he claims to have felt Reiki's energy for the first time. He was starving and close to death when he experienced a burst of intense healing energy. This gave him a renewed sense of vitality and heightened awareness that he had never felt before. He was compelled to open a clinic in Tokyo soon after to offer the healing modality. He taught the Reiki technique to more than 2000 people in his lifetime.

Reiki master Hawayo Takata began teaching Usui-Reiki in Hawaii in the 1930s, and it made its way to the mainland of the United States in the 1970s. It picked up fast, and by the mid-1990s, the technique was being used in hospitals around the United States. Many physicians, nurses, and other medical staff were trained to use Reiki, and it has grown exponentially since then. Today, Reiki is still used as a complementary treatment for surgery, cancer, and AIDS in hospitals and in private practices for multiple other issues, such as anxiety and depression.

Mikao Usui left us these words about the Reiki technique he developed. It reveals the heart and intention behind his teaching:

> "The secret art of inviting happiness.
>
> The miraculous medicine of all diseases.

Just for today, do not anger.

Do not worry and be filled with gratitude.

Devote yourself to your work. Be kind to people.

Every morning and evening, join your hands in prayer.

Pray these words to your heart and chant these words with your mouth:

Usui Reiki Treatment for the improvement of body and mind"

Chapter 3: The Benefits of Reiki

There are many incredible benefits of Reiki. Even though it's a simple process to learn and apply, it usually has profound effects. Reiki extends far beyond physical treatment. It also supports a healthy mind and spirit, allowing the client to experience a life that is more fulfilled and joyful.

Most people seek out Reiki when they are stressed, feeling some sort of energy imbalance, have physical illness or pain, or are going through a major transition. Others come for their spiritual development or to find a renewed sense of purpose. Many healthy individuals simply seek out Reiki treatment to maintain their happy sense of harmony.

Reiki is calming and relaxing, boosts energy, and opens the channels for a clear mind and balanced emotions. It provides us with a strong foundation to take on life's normal challenges with grace.

10 Benefits of Reiki

1. *Promotes Balance*

Reiki restores balance and promotes harmony in our physical, mental, emotional, and spiritual bodies. It's non-invasive and uses the body's natural healing ability to create an overall sense of well-being. As it works directly on balancing energy on all levels, it removes the blockages (which directly relate to various issues) instead of simply masking symptoms.

2. Creates Deep Relaxation

Reiki helps the body release stress and tension. The client is given time to themselves where they can simply lie down and "be." The practitioner performs the treatment, and as the client's body responds, they start to feel lighter and at peace. Reiki raises your awareness to subtle energies in your body and mind. You learn the language of your own body and are able to make wiser and more intuitive decisions. This feeling of being more mindfully present in your own body creates a profound sense of calm.

3. Dissolves Energy Blocks

When natural balance is restored between the mind, body, and soul, it results in a more peaceful state of being. Energy flows more freely and pain is released. As blocks are removed, clients often find that their thinking is clearer, their memory improves, and their emotional wounds are soothed. Reiki can calm mood swings, subdue fears, and soften feelings of anger and frustration. As energy is shifted, it impacts personal relationships and improves interactions with family, friends, and colleagues.

4. Detoxification and Immune Support

Reiki helps the body cleanse itself of toxins. Due to our stressful lifestyles, we are often in a reactive fight or flight response. This puts a heavy load on our immune system and can leave us feeling drained, irritable, and prone to sickness. Reiki shifts our body into healing mode, improves our digestion, helps clear our thoughts, and boosts our immunity. It is a highly beneficial modality when it comes to treating burn-out and adrenal fatigue.

5. Improves Focus

Reiki helps to clear the mind, and makes you feel grounded and centered. It can strengthen your ability to concentrate on tasks and be more productive. Reiki often has a positive effect on work and career performance.

6. Improves Sleep

The relaxation effects of a Reiki treatment lead directly to better sleep. Clients are able to fall asleep in the evenings more easily, overcome insomnia, and wake up feeling refreshed. They may even fall asleep during treatment.

7. Accelerates the Body's Self-Healing

Reiki returns the body to its natural, harmonious state. Breathing, heart rate, digestion, and blood pressure normalize and improve. One of the first things to happen in a Reiki session is that the client's breathing becomes deeper and easier. When our breath deepens, our minds settle, and our body heals.

8. Relieves Pain

Reiki can be targeted to relieve specific pain, such as injuries, migraines, arthritis, and sciatica. It can also help with physical ailments, such as asthma, chronic fatigue, menopausal symptoms, and menstrual pain.

9. Emotional Healing

Reiki leads to spiritual growth and development, and it can also help with healing deep trauma and emotional issues, such as depression and anxiety. Reiki addresses the whole person and can create tremendous shifts from deep within your being. Making decisions becomes easier, difficult emotions are managed more effectively (such as grief), and it can lead to an inspirational shift in attitudes and beliefs that may have held you back before. You are able to see your life from a fresh and positive perspective.

10. Complements Medical Treatment

We still need conventional medicine (e.g., insulin for diabetes), and there are a number of other therapies (such as counseling) that are beneficial. What makes Reiki so special is that it not only complements these treatments but actually enhances their effect. Reiki is non-invasive and gentle, requiring no physical touch. It can support a range of medical conditions and treatments, including epilepsy, heart conditions, chemotherapy, and pregnancy.

After learning about all the benefits of Reiki, you may be interested in finding out how you can become a practitioner yourself. In the next chapter, we'll have a look at the different levels of Reiki practitioners and what the training involves for each one.

Chapter 4: Reiki Practitioner Levels

Reiki practitioners are trained in three Reiki levels (also known as degrees).

There are a multitude of Reiki schools, and each has its own teachers and masters. They all explain and teach Reiki in their own unique way. The attunements are therefore offered from different perspectives, and there are some that still follow the ancient Japanese tradition.

Reiki was originally taught by a master as a whole and was split into different levels many decades later. In the beginning, there was no strict system, and it wasn't segmented in any way.

Each level of Reiki serves its own purpose. Just because a practitioner is at level one, it doesn't mean they are weaker or less capable of channeling energy. The degrees are merely a way for us to assimilate Reiki knowledge systematically. The student has a gradual and linear progression to mastery.

The different Reiki levels each represent a spiritual and energetic leap toward a higher level of awareness, knowledge, and consciousness.

The Purpose of Attunement

Attunement is when Reiki energy is passed from a master to a student. This connects the student to the universal Reiki source and qualifies you to be a vessel of Reiki energy. You then have the capability of moving this energy for yourself and others. You can't practice this healing art unless you have had an attunement, even if you know all the theory and hand positions.

What an Attunement Feels Like

Receiving an attunement is a powerful, life-altering spiritual experience. Your energetic pathways are opened by a Reiki master and strong universal energy flows freely through your body. Although the feelings and sensations differ from person to person, students report feeling lighter after their attunement and tingling all over their body.

The attunement enhances other energetic healing, and some students receive a heightened sense of intuitive awareness and psychic sensitivity.

Attunements at Each Level

Each Reiki school has their own method of passing on attunements at each level or degree. Some prefer to do so in the traditional way while others have adapted a modern approach. You may receive multiple attunements at each level, or you may only have one attunement for all three levels at once.

It's dependent on the Reiki master or teacher how they have chosen to pass on the healing technique of Reiki to their students. However, it's important to note that it doesn't really matter how many attunements you receive or how they were performed. It isn't the human being who attunes you. The master is merely a vessel through which the universal energy flows.

The attunements and their energy are passed from master to student through a sequence of techniques to open your body's main energetic channels and centers so that you can receive the universal life force energy.

During your attunements, you will receive different symbols at different stages. These symbols represent different aspects of

Reiki energy: power, mental and emotional balance, and distance healing.

The Three Reiki Levels

Reiki Level One (Shoden)

Level one (called *shoden* in Japanese) includes the beginner teachings of Reiki.

The student is taught the foundational Reiki principles:

- The hands-on technique: how to work on your own body and how to do self-treatment.

- An introduction to the 21 days, which is an essential and important concept of Reiki practice.

- A spiritual encounter and communication with spirit guides.

Level one is where the student learns how to work with themselves. They become accustomed to the different stages of vibration in the physical, emotional, and energetic body.

The student experiences what it feels like to be a channel of the universal life force energy and how it uniquely expresses itself in them. They will also experience deep healing in their own minds and bodies, cleanse blockages in their energy field, and will reach a higher state of awareness and consciousness.

Level one is an introspective process of inquiry. The student learns where they need healing and balancing, and they are able to direct their own energy to achieve this end.

Reiki Level Two (Okuden)

Level two (called *okuden* in Japanese) incorporates the inner hidden teachings.

Level one focused on your body and how to work with oneself from a physical and energetic perspective. Level two shifts toward mental activity and the emotions.

At this second degree, the student gains access to a higher vibration and experiences a stronger flow of universal energy. This leads to a sharper awareness of their mental balance (or imbalance) and current emotional state.

Channeling of energy is now not just through the physical body but also through time, space, and the emotional body.

The following is covered in level two:

- Heightened awareness and a higher vibration (usually accompanied by an attunement)

- An introduction to the sacred Reiki symbols. These include the symbols of power, mental-emotional healing, and distance. They may also include non-traditional symbols that are used for healing the heart and communication.

- How to use symbols for energizing and cleansing.

- How to transmit and channel energy through distance, time, and space.

- How to cleanse a room or space before practicing Reiki.

- How to create a Reiki project.

Reiki Level Three (Shinpiden)

Level three (called *shinpiden* in Japanese) is also known as the mystery teachings. It is considered by many schools of Reiki as the Master Degree.

This third degree includes:

- An enhanced ability to channel universal energy.

- A deep understanding of what a Reiki master is and what their responsibilities are.

- An introduction to the master symbol and the vibration it carries.

- A deep meditation with the master symbol.

At this level, the student has tremendous potential for a spiritual awakening and is considerably more adept at channeling universal life force energy.

In the next chapter, we will take a more in-depth look at each level as it relates to training to be a Reiki practitioner and becoming a master.

Chapter 5: How to Become a Reiki Practitioner

To become a Reiki practitioner who works with other people or animals, you need to have studied Reiki to at least level two.

We will now take a much closer look at each of the levels and what the training involves. The exact details of each course and level will differ according to which Reiki master you work with and which school of Reiki you sign up for. However, they will all cover much of the same information and preparation.

Practitioner Level One

As you'll remember from the previous chapter, the first level of training involves the beginner teachings where you'll learn the basic Reiki principles, the hands-on technique, how to communicate with your spirit guides, and how to use the energy of Reiki on yourself.

The Reiki Principles

These are the Reiki principles you will be introduced to in level one. You'll need to recite them every morning, night, and each and every time you practice Reiki. This helps to clear your energy and give you a sense of calm before you do any healing work.

- Just for today, I will be grateful.

- Just for today, I will not anger.

- Just for today, I will not worry.

- Just for today, I will do my work honestly.

- Just for today, I will respect all life.

The Initiation Ceremony

This ceremony is usually performed before you start your training and includes attunements from a master Reiki practitioner.

You'll be advised to not consume alcohol or drugs for at least two full days before the ceremony, as these substances can block the flow of your energy. Ideally, you will also avoid eating any meat, fish, or processed foods for 24 hours before the initiation, as digestion takes up a lot of your physical energy. Proteins and junk food rob you of the vital energy you need to fully experience the universal flow inside you.

The initiation ceremony is considered a sacred ritual. The Reiki master will use ancient symbols and mantras to connect you, the student, to the universal life force energy.

After your initiation and first attunement, you'll probably start to feel energy flow through your hands. This is the foundation of all your future Reiki healing.

The Hands-On Method

In level one, you'll learn the hands-on method of healing. Your hands will be activated during your initiation, and during the training, you'll learn how to place them in different positions to get a sense of what that feels like in your body.

You'll learn how to channel healing energy through your entire body and how to remove negative energy. The various positions of your hands will correspond to the main energy centers, channels, and chakras in your body. This creates a strong flow that you'll slowly become aware of as you move deeper through your training. This flow should ideally start from your head and then move downwards so that all the unwanted toxins and energy can eventually leave your body into the ground.

The 21-Day Cleanse

Following your initiation, you'll immediately start a 21-day detoxification and cleansing ritual. The attunement you receive from the master practitioner will be profoundly healing and activate all seven chakras in your body. It will also result in your body and mind releasing toxins and negative energy. The period of 21 days is chosen because it symbolizes the period of meditation that the founder, Mikao Usui, originally experienced.

Your body will naturally start cleansing itself, and you may experience physical symptoms of this detoxification (such as a runny nose, diarrhea, dizziness, or headaches). Your physical body is being prepared as a healing vessel and your entire system is readjusted, recalibrated, and rebalanced.

These 21 days should not be feared but rather used as a time of deep self-reflection and healing. If you feel any aches or pains during this powerful cleanse, you can place your hands on those areas and use the Reiki energy to ease your discomfort and speed up your healing.

This cleansing happens on all levels, not just physically. Your emotions may also be affected during this time, depending on your personal blockages, trauma, or scars. If you feel as if you need to cry, scream, or shout, then that is what you need to do. Some people feel very little or may simply feel more tired than usual and find that they yawn all the time. Others are the opposite, feeling hyper-energized and full of ideas.

Although it can be exhausting and mentally draining, this process is essential for your development as a Reiki practitioner. You need to be rid of the toxic energy that may have been holding you back your entire life. You will feel so much lighter afterwards. Reiki can give you a sense of rebirth. You simply need to trust the process.

Reiki holds its own form of wisdom, and your body and spirit will know what you need to work through during your cleanse. You may also experience this healing energy in your dreams as your subconscious mind processes different issues. If you get into the habit of giving yourself a Reiki treatment before you fall asleep and upon waking in the morning, you will have even more profound and insightful dreams.

Different Energy Sensations

Some people are disappointed during level one because they "can't feel anything." The detection of energy is a skill that needs to be learned, and this level of sensation differs from person to person.

There are three types of people:

- Extra sensitive— These students can feel the slightest change in their energy fields and those of others. They can describe the sensation in detail and are often immediately able to detect energy moving through their bodies and hands.

- Normal sensitive— These students can sense the energy flow but can't pick up on small fluctuations. It may feel more like a vague idea or a slight tingling sensation. You may wonder if you're imagining the energy because it appears to come and go.

- Insensitive— These students struggle to feel the flow of energy, especially in the beginning. However, over time, you can learn to pick up on the subtle shifts in your body and gradually become more attuned to how you individually detect the universal life force. Remember— it is always there, it's just a matter of finding your unique way of sensing it.

An Introduction to Your Spirit Guides

An essential aspect to level one, and in fact, to your entire Reiki training, is learning how to work with your spirit guides. These are positive, energetic entities from a higher plane of existence. Some people see them as angels or a form of deity while others perceive the spirit guide as a feeling or force.

It is believed that we each receive a spirit guide (or more than one) when we are born, but over time, we forget that they exist and lose our communication with them. When you receive your first attunement in level one, you'll also be reconnected to your spirit guides.

They are there to enhance your intuition and your sense of energy, as well as the ability you have to channel that energy for healing. Spirit guides can make your healing more powerful because they can help with certain activities (such as distance healing).

Practitioner Level Two

In the previous chapter, we mentioned that level two is all about the inner hidden teachings. This focuses on the mental and emotional parts of Reiki, channeling energy through time and space, and learning how to use sacred Reiki symbols.

We'll now take a closer look at these Reiki symbols and how they are used.

The Reiki Symbols

There are six ways to use Reiki symbols:

1. Visualize the symbol in the form of a bright, white image projecting from your third eye chakra (your forehead area) onto your hands as they rest above different areas of your client's body. This can be done with all the different Reiki hand positions and shapes.

2. Imagine a brilliant white symbol on your palms before you place them on or above your client.

3. Using your tongue, draw the symbol on the roof of your mouth. Now, project it from here onto the backs of your hands as you hover them above the client's body.

4. Once again, draw the symbol on the roof of your mouth with your tongue, and then project it onto your palms before placing your hands on or above the client.

5. Draw the symbol on your palms using your index fingers. Then, proceed to place your hands on or above the client.

6. Draw the symbol in the air with your index finger in the direction you wish the Reiki energy to flow.

It's important that you don't allow anyone, apart from a second-level student or master practitioner, to see the symbols you draw.

The drawn symbols need to be activated by silently repeating the words of the symbol, for example: Cho Ku Rei. Ideally, they are repeated three times.

It's possible to write out a problem or issue and then draw the symbol over it. As before, it's important to intone the symbol silently at the same time to activate its power. Place this paper between your palms for a few minutes to channel your energy through the problem to clear it.

Symbols can be sewn into clothes, sent under stamps on a letter, placed under a sticker on a gift, drawn onto plants, used on food and drinks, and drawn on the inside of your wallet, cell phone, or laptop. They can also be drawn (invisibly) under doormats, behind doors, and inside cupboards. The only limit is your imagination.

Cho Ku Rei (CKR)

The Cho Ku Rei Reiki symbol is the one that has the most uses and applications. It translates as "All the power of the universe, right here, right now."

"Cho" means "to cut." It removes illusions and allows you to see the whole.

"Ku" means "penetrating." You can imagine it as a sword slicing through something.

"Rei" means "universal." It represents omnipresence, or the ability to be everywhere at the same time.

CKR is capable of concentrating a tremendous amount of energy into one point and promotes healing, cleansing, and protection. CKR enhances the ability to channel universal energy and can feel as if you're flipping a light switch on. CKR cuts through resistance and helps to remove barriers. This symbol can be used and activated on different energy centers on the body or simply on your palms for an optimal flow of energy. It also activates the other symbols.

The Cho Ku Rei symbol looks like this:

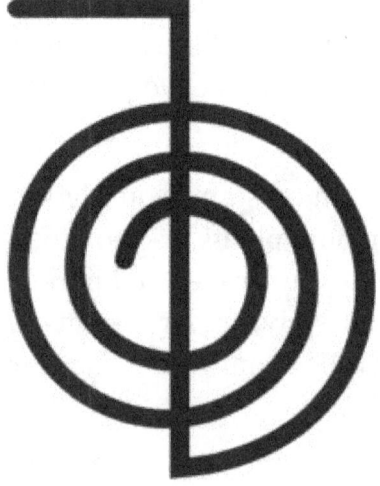

Examples of situations where the CKR symbol can be used include the following:

- To activate other symbols.

- To cleanse energy in a room.

- To set up a layer of protection.

- To bring balance to your body, emotions, or home.

Sei Hei Ki (SHK)

The Sei Hei Ki symbol represents healing at a mental and emotional level. It brings harmony and balance to situations. It can be used to open a dimension, to cleanse the subconscious, and for emotional healing. In therapy, it is useful for clearing negative and self-sabotaging thoughts. SHK can also be used to activate energy centers and channels or to help with getting over addictions.

"Sei" means "birth." It represents coming into being and the act of creation.

"Heiki" means "balance." It represents finding equilibrium.

The Sei Hei Ki symbol looks like this:

Examples of where the SHK symbol is used effectively include:

- It works on physical blockages and resistance.

- It helps with addictions, phobias, and eating disorders.

- It works on a range of emotions, such as anxiety, fear, sadness, and grief.

- It can improve your memory and intuition.

- It calms negative atmospheres.

- It balances energies in the home, workplace, and healing tools, such as crystals.

- It can calm arguments and relieve tension.

- It improves poor communication.

- It protects you and your belongings while traveling.

- It can help you find things you have lost.

- It helps people with head injuries or who are in a coma.

Hon Sha Ze Sho Nen (HSZSN)

This is the distance healing tool and is considered one of the most interesting symbols in Reiki. It can help you transcend time and space when sending energy. It is usually used in conjunction with the first two symbols in a specific sequence: CKR-SHK-HSZSN. This makes it possible to send healing energy to the past, present, future, and across vast distances.

The Hon Sha Ze Sho Nen symbol looks like this:

The HSZSN symbol can be used for the following purposes:

- It works on deeply rooted issues (such as childhood abuse).

- It can channel Reiki energy to someone in a different part of the world.

- It can work on large groups of people at once.

- It can help with large-scale disasters (such as a tsunami).

- It works towards success in exams and interviews.

- It can help resolve karmic issues from past lives.

- It can work on people while they are asleep.

- It crosses all perceived boundaries of time and space.

Shika-So

The Shika-So symbol is mainly used for the throat energy center. It can assist with healing a wide range of physical afflictions and also enhances the client's communication skills. The Shika-So symbol helps us express deep and repressed emotions, and it also promotes harmonious relationships with the people we interact with.

Shika-Sei Ki

This powerful symbol is mostly used for the heart chakra. It helps release emotional blockages and provides stress relief. The Shika-Sei Ki symbol is of particular benefit in relationship healing and restoration, as well as for physical heart conditions.

Practitioner Level Three

The most important part of the third level is to learn the master symbol and master the attunement process. This allows you to teach the gift and technique of Reiki to other students.

It's important to know that once you have reached level three and attained master status, it is only the beginning of your journey. The third degree doesn't suddenly make you wiser and more powerful. You still have to continually work on your personal and spiritual development.

The only prerequisite (apart from completion of level one and two) is that you have a true desire to help others.

The Master Symbol: Dai Ko Myo (DKM)

This is the most powerful symbol in Reiki and can only be used by master practitioners. Its purpose is to heal the soul or spirit, and it does this by reaching the original source of pain in the aura or energy field. It improves intuition and psychic abilities and can result in major life transformations.

Dai Ko Myo means "great shining light" and represents the divine. The DKM symbol is also known as the satori symbol. It is used in Buddhism and you will often see it written in Buddhist temples.

Master Reiki practitioners use this symbol during initiation and attunement of their students. Many people find their true calling and life purpose after using this symbol and it can be a catalyst for major changes.

This is what the Dai Ko Myo symbol looks like:

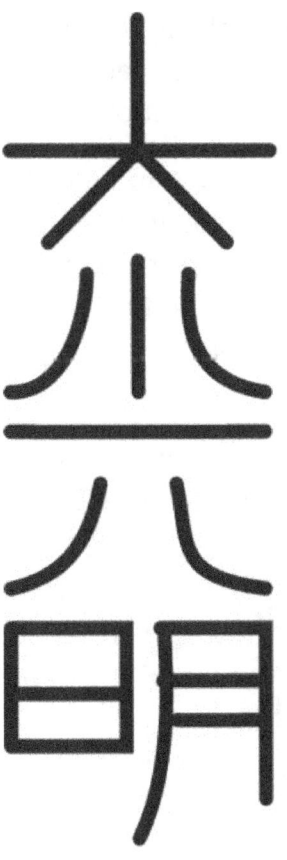

The Reiki Attunement Ceremony

During level three training, you will learn how to conduct attunements. After an attunement ceremony, your students will be able to channel the universal life force energy. It is a permanent gift, and the ability lasts for a lifetime.

Attunement does not, however, magically transform a student into a healer. The student simply becomes a vessel for Reiki energy.

Attunement processes, symbols, and ceremonies differ from master to master. This doesn't make a difference because the universal energy will flow regardless. What is most important is that the student is relaxed and open with a strong desire to receive the attunement and work with healing Reiki energy. The master should likewise be calm and hold a pure intention.

Reiki attunements are simple and only take a few minutes to perform. Usually, the student is asked to remove their shoes and any jewelry, and they then sit on a chair with their feet flat on the floor. Their hands are held in a prayer position, and the master Reiki practitioner follows their intuition as they perform the attunement.

After training to be a practitioner, you can start performing Reiki treatments. We will take a closer look at what this involves in the next chapter.

Chapter 6: Reiki Healing Sessions

Reiki can be used to treat yourself and others (including animals). It can be performed from a distance or through hands-on healing. We'll take a deep dive into each of these now.

Treating Yourself

After completing level one, you will have connected with the universal life force energy and felt it move through you. You are now ready to work on your own body and be a channel for your personal healing.

This is the perfect and safest place to practice what you have learned. You will be able to detect any changes and will know what these energy changes feels like in your body. Later, when you explain the process to your clients or students, you will have a clear idea of what it personally feels like to feel an energy shift and to notice subtle differences.

Your first few months after going through the first degree are an ideal time to learn the Reiki skills and gain confidence by practicing on yourself. The more you practice the techniques, the more accurate your intuition will become.

Reiki will not only help you with self-healing but can also serve as a protective tool and a way to develop emotionally and mentally. You can use Reiki on yourself every day, especially when you are feeling ill, stressed, tired, anxious, or have any kind of ache or pain. When you lay your hands on your body, Reiki's infinite wisdom will do the rest.

Reiki recharges your batteries, brings balance, and provides clarity and peace of mind. You will find that your self-esteem improves over time and that you'll be more comfortable in your own skin. You'll be more patient with normal daily stressors and most likely be a wonderful person to be around!

The more you use Reiki energy, the stronger it becomes.

Benefits of Self-Treatment

- Promotes relaxation and decreases stress
- Centers and clarifies thoughts
- Energizes you when you are exhausted or drained
- Can calm you down if you are frightened or anxious
- Focuses your mind and helps you find solutions to problems
- Relieves physical pain
- Accelerates natural healing of wounds and illnesses
- Improves health and boosts immunity
- Gradually relieves chronic problems (such as irritable bowel syndrome)
- Helps prevent diseases
- Detoxifies the body
- Dissolves blockages in energy
- Helps heal emotional wounds and trauma
- Turns around negative thinking

How to Treat Yourself

There is no right or wrong way of working with Reiki energy on yourself. Your intuition will gradually become stronger the more you practice, and you'll know where and how to place your hands with experience. In the beginning, it will simply be trial and error, and you should follow what feels most right for you.

If you are aware of a particular problem, such as a sore knee, then place your hands directly over that area, and then follow that with a full body treatment. It's important to drink some water afterwards and to pay attention to your thoughts and feelings. You may feel light-headed or perhaps like you need to sleep. Follow what you feel your body needs. Always listen to your intuition.

There are different hand positions that you can immediately master, and you'll usually spend three to five minutes in each place during a self-healing Reiki session.

Self-Treatment Hand Positions

One full treatment involves moving through these hand positions in the following sequence (from the top of the body downwards).

1. Cup your hands over your eyes, cheekbones, and forehead. This can help ease stress, eye issues, asthma, headaches, allergies, and mental or emotional disturbances.

2. Place your hands on top of your head with your fingers touching, as if you're holding a crown on your head. This relieves headaches, migraines, stress, multiple sclerosis, strong or negative emotions, and digestive disorders.

3. Place your hands on either side of your head with your palms on your temples and your fingers resting on the top of your head. This helps with balance, tinnitus, earache, and colds.

4. Place your hands at the back of your head just above your neck. Allow your fingertips to touch. This relieves headaches, fears, phobias, and depression.

5. Cover your hands over the tops of your shoulders and base of the neck. This position helps for aches and pains, stress, tension, tight muscles, and shock.

6. Place your hands around your neck with the base of your palms touching at your throat. This assists with communication, self-expression, sore throat, speech problems, bronchitis, breathing difficulty, anger, and voice loss.

7. This position is over your chest. Place your left hand just below the sternum (heart area) with your palm facing your chest and fingers pointing upwards. Place your right hand above your left in a T-position. Your fingers will point toward the left, with the tips of your left hand's fingers brushing against the pinky of your right hand. Your right hand is now covering your thymus gland. This position helps with heart problems, angina, breathing problems, thyroid and weight problems, immune system, lymph flow, emotional problems, and stress. It is fantastic for calming down when you're anxious.

8. Place your hands horizontally just above your chest or breasts. Your fingertips can touch.

9. Move your hands (same orientation) to just below the chest or breasts, approximately in line with your

diaphragm. Positions eight and nine send healing energy to all the major organs, treat disease and infection, and help with stomach issues, anger, and emotions.

10. The hands are positioned horizontally across the navel area (center of the stomach).

11. Position your hands in a V-shape (fingers pointing downwards) on the inside of your hip bone. This will form an upside-down triangle at the lowest part of your abdominal area (your thumbs and forefingers almost touch). Positions 10 and 11 send healing energy to all major organs and glands, stomach, intestines, reproductive organs, and serve to calm anger, and emotions.

12. Cup the hands over the top of the knees (fingers will face towards your shins).

13. Place hands behind the back of the knees. You can also do position 12 and 13 at the same time on one knee, then do the other side, if this is more comfortable. These hand positions help with knee and leg pain, varicose veins, mobility issues, and poor circulation.

14. Position your hands on top of your shoulders, touching your shoulder blades.

15. Place your hands horizontally in the center of your back, as high as physically comfortable. Try to get as close as you can to the bottom of your shoulder blades. Position 14 and 15 target major organs and glands, spinal problems, and stress.

16. Position your hands at the bottom of your back in a horizontal position. You'll feel them just below your rib cage.

17. Place your hands in a V-shape at the base of your spine. Positions 16 and 17 send healing to all the major organs, treat infections, back and spinal problems, and stress.

18. Sit with the soles of your feet touching and hold both feet with your hands. This helps with leg pain, varicose veins, and works on all the reflexology points on the feet.

Treating Others

Before you treat others, it's important to remember the following:

- Don't give treatments to people with pacemakers, as the Reiki energy can alter their rhythms.

- Be very careful with clients who have diabetes and are taking insulin injections. They will need to check their insulin levels because Reiki may reduce the amount of insulin they require.

- Be very clear with your clients about what they can expect during a treatment session, as well as possible symptoms that may arise in the days following. Here are some typical reactions and experiences that can occur during a session:

  o A sensation of heat or cold

  o Pins and needles

  o Lots of vivid colors in their mind's eye

- Flashes from a past life

- Involuntary movements

- Slight muscle spasms or jerks

- They may fall asleep

- Itchiness

- Various emotional responses

- Rumbling stomach

- Flood of memories

- They may sense your hands moving

- They may even feel nothing at all

- Reiki travels to the area that it is needed most. Don't try to think ahead or force the energy to go somewhere. Just flow with it.

- Forget the symptoms and treat the whole person. Listen to your client's body and sense the shifts in energy as you work. Trust your intuition.

- Be aware of any non-verbal communication from your client. This includes sighing or slight twitches. They may also smile when something pleasant happens with their energy.

- Normally a session lasts between 60 and 90 minutes.

- Offer your client a glass of water after the treatment (this helps with grounding).

- Wash your hands under cold, running water after the session.

Preparing the Environment

You need to create a calm, peaceful area for practicing Reiki on others. The space should be light and feel safe. It needs to be clean and smell fresh, and you can paint the walls in healing colors such as white, light yellow, or pale purple. Ensure that the room will be undisturbed, and that all distractions are turned off (e.g., cell phones).

It is a good idea to invest in a therapy table. You'll need two pillows— one for the client's head and one for their feet. Always have a warm blanket available, as we tend to feel cold after lying down for a while.

To increase positive energy in the room, you can add a few house plants and possibly a collection of appropriate crystals. You can work in silence or add gentle background music. You can also use natural sounds, such as dolphin and whale calls, or gentle rain.

You can burn aromatic oils or incense. However, you need to make sure that your client doesn't have any allergies or sensitivities. Keep a box of tissues close by in case the person has an emotional release and starts to cry.

Ask the client to remove all their jewelry, their watch, and glasses. Metal can disrupt the flow of energy in some cases. Remember to also cleanse your gemstones and crystals on a regular basis, as they sometimes absorb negative energy.

Both you and your client need to wear loose-fitting clothing. Take off restrictive items such as belts, shoes, and ties. This not only makes you feel more relaxed and comfortable but also ensures an easy flow of energy between you.

You and your client should both avoid drinking alcohol for at least 24 hours before a session because it can dissipate your energy.

Always take care of your personal hygiene and smell clean and fresh. Avoid wearing strong perfume and refrain from eating food a few hours before that contains garlic or onion. Wash your hands before a session with a fragrance-free soap. Remember, your hands will be on (or near) your client's face, so it is essential to be clean and hygienic.

The Invocation

This is a silent prayer or mantra you say just before you start the session. You can take this opportunity to declare that you are simply a vessel and that any healing that takes place is through the power of the universal life force. Remember, you are not healing your clients— they are actually healing themselves!

You are the channel that helps to open up the energy and send Reiki healing energy toward places on the client's body that need it most. The invocation declares that you are a conduit and a vessel through which universal life flows. It's a humble sign of respect.

The prayer you choose is personal and should be in line with your own beliefs. Always ask for permission to be used as a channel for healing Reiki energy.

When your client is ready to start, have them lie down on the table with their eyes closed. Make sure they are completely relaxed before you begin.

Move to the top of the table (where the client's head is) and close your eyes as you join your hands together in a prayer position at the center of your chest. You can also place your hands on your client's shoulders. Make it your sincerest wish to pass on unconditional love and to channel healing energy. You can also invite your spirit guides into the room to help you with the session.

Cleanse the Client's Aura

Before you start the Reiki treatment, run your hands along your client's aura approximately six inches above their body. Move slowly from their head to their feet. Do this at least three times. This movement removes any superficial energy blockages and brings a sense of harmony to the aura. This initial flow over your client's body is a perfect opportunity to feel their body's energy with your intuition. You may already pick up where there are knots of strangled energy. You can focus on these areas in the healing session.

The Full Reiki Treatment

Have your client lie on the therapy table with their arms at their sides and eyes closed. Make sure that their legs aren't crossed and are flat against the table. This ensures an optimal flow of energy.

Gently lay your hands on or above your client's body in the different positions you were taught, which I will expand on shortly (for three to five minutes in each place). Move on when you feel the energy getting less or when your intuition guides you to.

Your hands should be cupped with your fingers together. This keeps the energy flowing smoothly. In sensitive areas (such as breasts, genitals, wounds, and burns) keep your hands above the body and don't ever allow them to touch.

Reiki Hand Positions (Front)

Move in the following sequence with your hands (unless your intuition guides you otherwise):

1. Cup your hands and rest them over your client's eyes, forehead, and cheekbones.

2. Place your hands on the client's head with your palms touching at the top of the head and your fingertips slightly above the ears.

3. Place your hands on either side of your client's head (over their ears) with your fingers covering their temples and extending to their jawline.

4. Gently move your client's head to one side, placing one hand on the back of the head (just above the neck). Now move the head to the opposite side, placing your hand on the other side of the back of the head.

5. After gently moving your client's head to remove your hands, much like you did in the previous step, place your hands along the bottom of their jaw. Your fingertips will touch with your thumbs gently resting on their chin. Your hands are essentially cupping the bottom of their cheeks here.

6. Position your hands on the top of your client's shoulders, fingers pointing downwards along their upper arm.

7. Place your hands in a T-shape on or above your client's chest. Your right hand will be just below the sternum, fingers pointing upwards. Your left hand will cross just above that to form a T.

8. Position your hands horizontally below the breast line. Both hands will face the same direction.

9. Move your hands slightly lower, still horizontal, above the navel.

10. With care and respect, without touching your client's body, place your left hand above their right hip crease (your fingers will point downwards) and your right hand above their left hip crease (fingers facing up). Your hands will form a V-shape.

11. Gently place your hands on your client's knees.

12. Finally, place one hand on each foot. Afterwards, ask your client to turn over. Remember to ask this quietly and gently, as they may have fallen asleep or be in a deep state of relaxation.

Reiki Hand Positions (Back)

13. Place your hands horizontally (both hands facing the same direction) on the client's upper back (on top of the shoulder blades).

14. Keeping your hands in the same horizontal shape, move a couple of inches lower to just below their shoulder blades.

15. Once again, keeping the shape, move a few inches lower. Your hands will be just below their ribs.

16. Move a couple of inches lower again, placing your hands on their lower back (above the kidneys).

17. Make a T-position with your hands. Your right hand will rest above the sacrum (between the "butt cheeks") with fingers facing upwards. Your left hand will form a horizontal line above this (on the client's lower back), with fingers pointing away from you.

18. Place your hands on the backs of your client's knees.

19. Finally, place a hand on the sole of each foot.

Once you have gone through all the hand positions, place your left hand on your client's crown chakra (on the top of the head) and your right hand at the base of their spine. This balances the energy in your client's body.

To seal off the practice, comb your client's aura. You do this by stroking the body firmly from the crown of the head to the feet in a sweeping motion. Continue past the feet to the floor to ground the energy. Repeat a second time, just lightly touching the body. Finally, do a third sweep hovering just above the physical body in the aura field.

Reiki From a Distance

When performing Reiki from a distance, the most important skill you have is your intuition. You won't be receiving instant feedback from the client, and unlike in-person treatment, you won't be able to observe the person's body and reactions. There is no way to know if they are crying, sighing, moving, or showing any subtle non-verbal communication.

That being said, distance healing with Reiki is certainly possible.

Structure of a Distance Reiki Session

1. Ask Permission

This may sound obvious, but it's extremely important. Sometimes clients are too ill and unable to talk, and other times someone has asked for healing on their behalf. However, the individuals themselves need to acknowledge in some way that they are happy with you using Reiki energy on them. This is ethical and essential for your integrity as a Reiki practitioner.

2. Use a Photograph

You can request a photograph of the client and hold this in your cupped hands (image facing upwards). You can now visualize and imagine the following Reiki symbols on top of the photograph (say each one aloud three times as you do so):

- Cho Ku Rei (power symbol)
- Sei Hei Ki (emotional symbol)
- Hon Sha Ze Sho Nen (distance symbol)

Now say the client's name aloud three times as you close your hands and cover the photo.

3. Imagine Being in the Room

Visualize yourself being in the room with this person and that they are either sitting in a chair or lying on a bed, ready to receive the treatment. In your mind's eye, draw the three symbols again (while intoning the names of the symbols), this time, onto the body of the client.

Using your imagination, conduct a full Reiki session in your mind. Move your hands as you would if you were in the room. Pay special attention to any trouble areas you are intuitively drawn to or what the client may have mentioned beforehand.

Once the full session is complete, cleanse the client's aura and ground them. Wash your hands with cold, running water and thank your spirit guides. Remember to ground yourself afterwards as well.

Interestingly, the founder of Reiki, Dr. Mikao Usui, preferred the distant healing method. He called it "Enkaku Chiryo Ho" which means "remote treatment method."

In the chapter on advanced Reiki techniques, we will look at distance healing on entirely different levels, including entire towns and countries.

For now, however, we'll look more closely at the individual client and learn more about basic anatomy and physiology.

Chapter 7: Anatomy for Reiki

Most clients that come to Reiki sessions are there to find relief from physical pain or illness. Although you don't need to know the body's anatomy and physiology in order to be a successful practitioner, it does help to know where the major organs and systems are so that you have a good idea where to lay your hands. This makes the whole process easier and quicker.

Reiki energy will naturally flow to the parts of the body that need it most, so you don't need to worry too much about remembering all the details. Use this simply as a guide that can help you.

The Endocrine System

This is the system that is responsible for releasing hormones into the body. It consists of ductless glands, and it works hand-in-hand with the nervous system. It helps to regulate metabolic activities and maintain homeostasis (balance) in the body.

The following diagram will give you a visual idea of where the various glands are located:

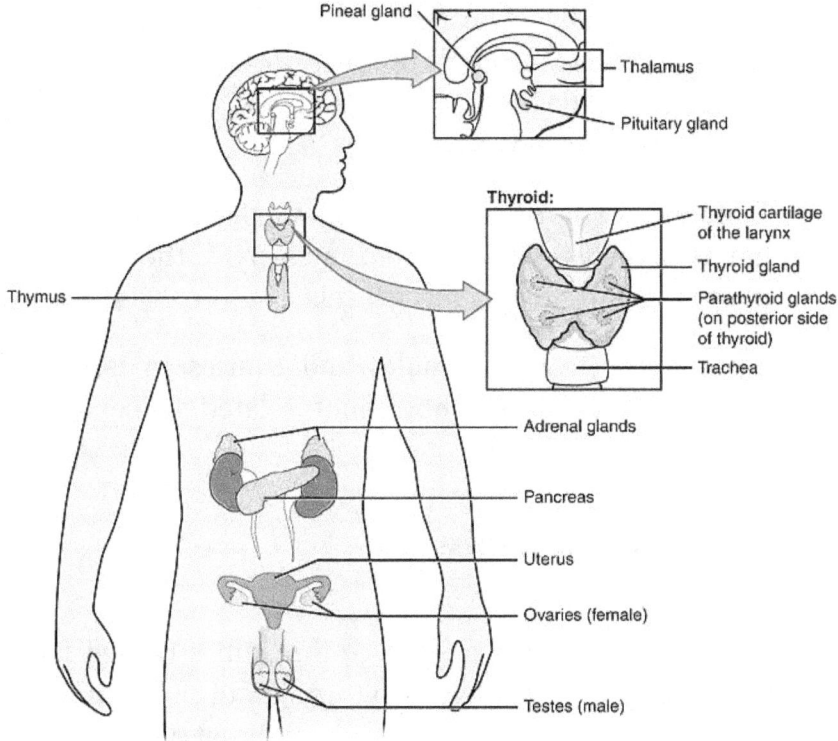

These are the primary endocrine glands:

- Pituitary gland— This pea-sized gland is found at the base of the brain and is vitally important because it controls all the other glands in the body.

- Thyroid gland— This butterfly-shaped organ is found in the neck and releases hormones that control metabolism. If you're always fatigued, there may be a problem with your thyroid gland.

- Parathyroid glands— There are four of these in the tissue that surrounds the back of the thyroid gland, and they are responsible for regulating calcium in our bodies.

- Adrenal glands— Located on top of the kidneys, these triangular-shaped glands produce hormones that regulate metabolism, the immune system, blood pressure, and the body's stress response.

- Pancreas— This organ has two main glands. The exocrine gland secretes digestive enzymes, and the endocrine gland regulates blood sugar levels.

- Sex glands (testes in males and ovaries in females)— These glands secrete hormones related to sexual and reproductive function.

The Lymphatic System

The lymphatic system is a system of thin tubes (called lymph vessels) that run like a massive web throughout the body. These vessels carry a milky liquid known as lymph that contains white blood cells, proteins, and fats.

The purpose of the lymphatic system is to protect your body against infection and to eliminate waste from the body. There are dozens of lymph nodes throughout your body, and when you're sick, you can feel that these are often tender and swollen (for example, in your neck, groin, and armpits). The largest lymph organ is the spleen.

If your client has an immune disorder or is constantly getting sick, check for swelling or pain in the lymph nodes and run your hands over these areas.

The following diagram will give you a sense of where the lymph nodes are located in the body:

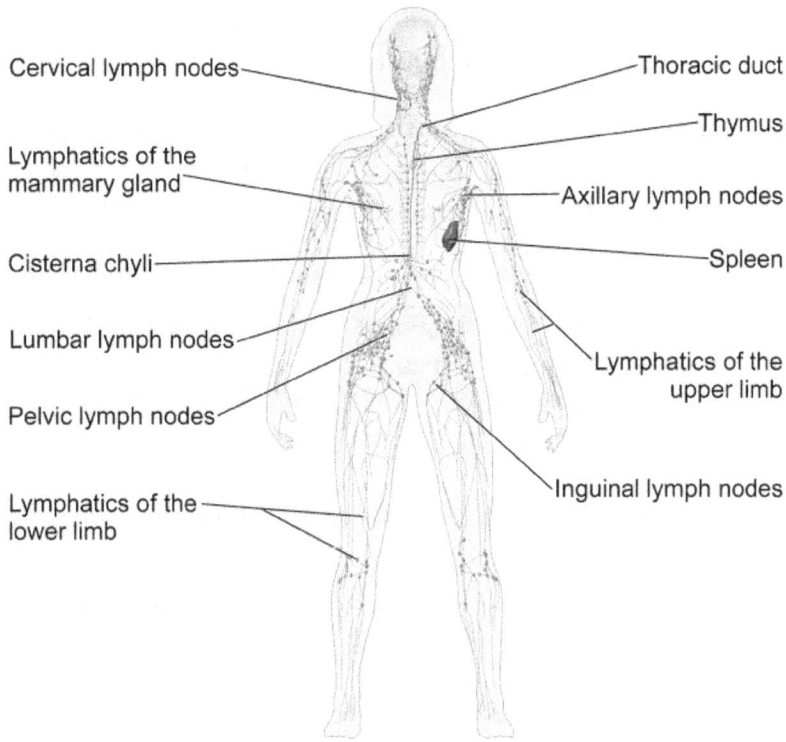

Cervical lymph nodes

Lymphatics of the mammary gland

Cisterna chyli

Lumbar lymph nodes

Pelvic lymph nodes

Lymphatics of the lower limb

Thoracic duct

Thymus

Axillary lymph nodes

Spleen

Lymphatics of the upper limb

Inguinal lymph nodes

The Internal Organs

If your client speaks about a history of problems with a particular organ, it helps to know where it is in the body. The basic anatomy is fairly easy to learn.

These are the main internal organs you should be aware of:

- Heart— The heart is what keeps us alive and is responsible for pumping blood around our body. Common client complaints include a racing heart, angina, chest pain, and previous heart surgery (such as a bypass). You can hover your hands just above the rib cage to channel universal healing energy to the heart.

- Lungs— These magnificent organs, along with the diaphragm, help us to breathe. Common client concerns include asthma, allergies, anxiety, panic attacks, and shortness of breath.

- Stomach— The place where our food is broken down with digestive enzymes. It is a highly acidic environment and common issues include acid reflux, stomach ulcers, and cramps.

- Small intestines and colon— The digestive tract is home to the microbiome which contains healthy bacteria that help us digest and process our food. Many people suffer from digestive issues such as constipation, bloating, diarrhea, and cramps.

- Bladder— This hollow organ in our lower abdomen stores urine. Common complaints include cystitis (inflammation), urinary tract infections (UTIs), and incontinence.

- Kidneys— We have two bean-shaped kidneys that are positioned in our lower back area, on either side of the spine. They transform waste into urine and remove toxins from the body. Issues can include kidney stones and cysts.

- Liver — This football-sized organ sits below our ribcage on the right side. It is our main detoxification organ. Liver problems can lead to jaundice, pain, and fatigue.

- Gallbladder— This is a small pouch located below the liver that stores bile. It is essential for digestion and transforming waste. Problems can include gallstones, nausea, and vomiting.

Here is a useful visual reference for the body's organs and where they are situated:

Internal organs

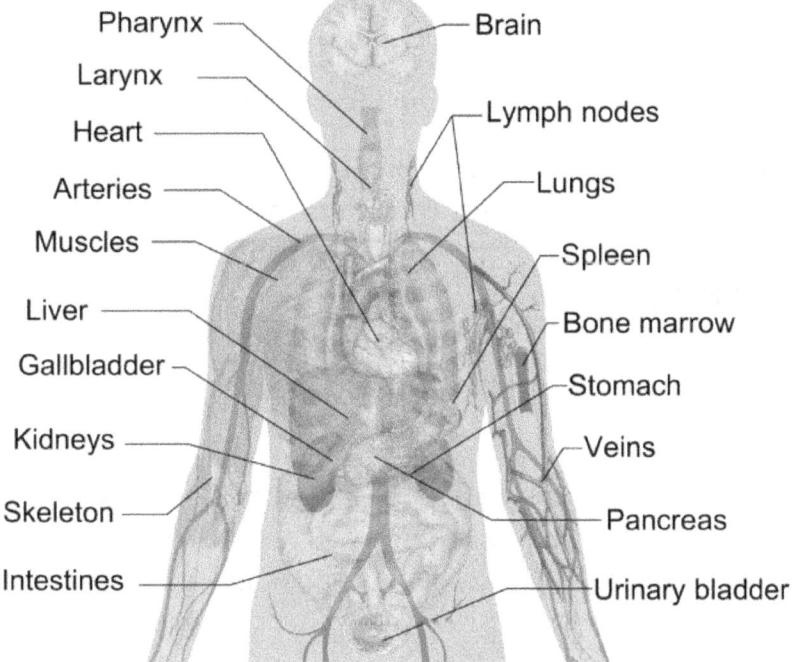

In the next chapter, we will look at the fascinating topic of other bodies and immerse ourselves in the world of animal Reiki.

Chapter 8: Animal Reiki

Animals are incredibly sensitive and receptive to Reiki energy. It can be used for stressed and anxious pets, animals that have been hurt, before an anxiety-inducing event such as international travel, after a traumatic event, or during periods of grief (when an owner has passed away, for instance). It can even be used just before an animal is put down so that the transition from life to death is a peaceful, calm, and loving experience.

Animals immediately relax during Reiki sessions, as they appear to be even more perceptive than humans to subtle changes in energy. Learning to work with Reiki and animals is an incredibly rewarding experience.

Developing a Relationship with the Animal

Different animals have different levels of pain and trauma, and their individual temperaments vary. Depending on their illness or condition, they may respond in a range of ways to Reiki treatment.

Developing a certain level of trust with this special being is essential. As you know, the client (in this case, an animal) needs to be completely relaxed for the Reiki energy to be effective. It may take time to develop a rapport with the animal, but it will definitely be worth it.

You'll usually be able to tell how an animal is feeling based on their behavior. If they bark, growl, screech, hiss, buck, or keep trying to get away, it is their way of telling you that they don't want you to touch them or get too close. You need to respect this, and then try to work from a distance through beaming or sending distant Reiki energy.

It's important to respect the animal's boundaries and to work in a calm and gentle manner.

Hands-On Animal Reiki

Once you sense that the animal is comfortable with you being close by, you can hover your hands just above their body and take note of their response. If they are still calm, then you can gradually move to gentle touch.

You will now adapt the hand positions and methods you learned in Reiki level one and two. Always approach slowly and move gently while continually observing their behavior. The animal may be cautious of your behavior in the beginning, but once they are aware that you're trying to help and will not harm them, most relax fairly quickly.

Remember to keep your intention pure and to state this in your mind throughout the session. Animals pick up on these thoughts and your energy.

The animal may also be incredibly comfortable with your hands-on healing, but then try to shift positions or change their expression. If this happens, allow them that little bit of space and hover your hands a few inches above their body again. Scan their aura and body and follow your intuition. Once the animal has settled, try to place your hands on them again and see what happens.

Sometimes, the animal moves when it senses what you are doing, and they try to move particular parts of their body towards your hands. If you pick up that this is happening, keep your hands in the same spot and allow the animal to move as it needs to. After they have adjusted and seem to be settled again, try to place your hands on their body and continue the treatment.

If you feel unsafe during the session (perhaps because the animal seems aggressive) or if the energy shifts and the animal seems uncomfortable, then always feel free to move away and do the treatment from a distance or stop altogether.

Effects of Animal Reiki

Most animals respond incredibly positively to Reiki sessions. They appear to sense the loving energy from the practitioner and pick up on subtle changes in their bodies. Many fall asleep and relax completely.

The positive changes in the animal, if it is a pet, often have a very positive effect on the owner or human companion too. This ripple effect of Reiki is fairly common, and it is of particular interest when performing Reiki on larger groups of individuals at the same time. This is what we will cover in the next chapter.

Chapter 9: Advanced Reiki

Once you are comfortable and confident with normal Reiki, you may wish to take it even further with some advanced techniques. These require lots of practice and greater levels of intuition. Even if you're not ready for them now, you may be interested in finding out how incredible it can get.

Sending Reiki Energy to the Future

Reiki can be sent to future important events such as a wedding, job interview, exam, competition, or doctor visit. You can send this Reiki energy to your future self or to someone else.

When you send the Reiki energy, you can stipulate the time and place, if you have that information. If, for example, your child is writing exams, you can print out their exam timetable and use this as your Reiki "prop" or "surrogate."

You place the surrogate item in your hands (just as you would do with a photograph of someone for distance healing) and visualize the three primary Reiki symbols as you repeat them in your mind. You can then say a prayer or state your intention as you focus the universal life force energy on that future event.

Sending Reiki Energy to the Past

You can't change events in history, but you can heal the results of what happened. We tend to hold onto past experiences and traumas, and much of what we seek healing for now is actually connected to processing that past pain. As a simple physical example, you may be struggling with persistent shoulder pain from an injury you sustained more than 10 years ago.

You can return to the scene of the injury or accident in your imagination and send healing Reiki energy to yourself. Set an intention for this specific past experience, visualize yourself going through that again, and then send the Reiki energy.

Sending Reiki to Yourself

Apart from physical hands-on techniques that you can easily perform on yourself at any time, you can also use distance healing on yourself. It sounds strange, but stay with me!

You can send healing Reiki energy to a moment in your past when you went through something traumatic, experienced an injury, or went through a tremendous loss (such as a break-up). When you send Reiki to the past, it can bring relief in the present. It will also help clear up blockages from those events that are still in your energy field. Healing the past can be cathartic and liberating.

You can also send Reiki to your future self. You can go one day or even several years into your future. It may be for a significant event, it could be for business success, or even for a nice relaxing vacation.

In the present moment, you may not be able to do hands-on healing for whatever reason. Perhaps you're on public transport, in your place of work, or waiting in a doctor's room. But you can still use Reiki! Perhaps you're feeling stressed, tired, or in need of an energy boost. All you need to do is close your eyes and imagine yourself in your mind's eye sending and receiving the Reiki energy. See and experience the healing white light, feel it enveloping your whole body, and imagine it flowing through your veins, muscles, and all of your energy channels.

You may receive confirmation or validation of this Reiki (to the past, present, or future) through a sound, voice in your head, a flashing image, or simply a new sense of calm and release.

Sending Reiki to Places and World Events

Reiki energy can be sent to any place, event, disaster, or world event. It can be absolutely anywhere in the world.

For example, you may wish to send healing vibrations to an area where a natural disaster has just taken place, such as an earthquake or flood. You can also send Reiki energy to specific parts of the world that need healing, such as oceans that are incredibly polluted or forests that are being destroyed. You can even send Reiki healing energy to scenes of horrible accidents (such as a train accident) or war zones.

You'll use the same distance healing techniques you learned before. Of course, you can't ask individual permission in these cases, so you'll need to trust that the universal Reiki energy will naturally flow where it is needed and wanted. You're not sending it to an individual but rather making the energy available to anyone who needs it and is open to its power.

Sending Reiki to Multiple People

It's not always possible to give all of your clients full individual sessions due to time constraints. For example, you may have dozens of international, distant clients who request Reiki healing every day. Instead of turning them all away, you can work with the energy in a different way.

It's possible to send Reiki to multiple people at the same time. You can combine several requests together and channel your energy simultaneously. It's much like typing an email and sending it to many people at the same time— the content and effect is the same; it's just going to many at once. You can help a number of people while still respecting your own time and energy resources.

There are a number of creative ways that you can do this:

- Reiki box or bowl— Write down the names of people or events on pieces of paper and place them inside a box, along with photographs and any other surrogate items. Send Reiki energy to the box or bowl regularly.

  You can place healing crystals in or around the box, and remember to always set a respectful and humble intention before each session. It's important to regularly go through the box and remove any clients or situations that no longer need Reiki.

- Crystal grid— You can charge various crystals with Reiki energy and place them in a healing grid. This is usually according to a set pattern. Crystals can enhance energy you send from a distance.

- Photo board— You can pin photographs and notes for people you are sending Reiki energy to on a bulletin board. You can stand in front of this and beam Reiki to them during your multiple-person Reiki treatment.

If you have any intuitive insights for specific people while you are doing the Reiki healing, be sure to tell them about it afterwards.

It's also good to ask for feedback every now and then so that you can be sure of the efficacy of your chosen methods.

Psychic Surgery

Our beliefs, attitudes, and emotions often hold us back from our full potential. The more ingrained these thoughts are, the more we tend to repeat them. If, for example, we have the belief that we will never have enough money, then each time something appears to confirm this in our life (perhaps our wallet is stolen or we don't get the raise we so desperately needed), then it reinforces that belief. This belief or unwanted, negative emotion (such as bitterness) can create a major block in our energy field. Psychic surgery is a Reiki technique that can help heal these deep afflictions.

These deep blockages in our life force usually have a particular shape or form and lodge themselves around certain organs, chakras, or even in the aura itself. They can cause health problems and many other difficulties.

When they are removed, the natural flow of energy can return, and the person can eventually return to optimal health.

Psychic surgery can be used to heal problems such as emotional difficulties, traumatic memories, relationship problems, addictions, and negative thoughts. It can be performed on yourself or a client.

Identify the Problem

The first step is to give the problem an identity or physical form in your mind's eye. This makes it easier to "see" and focus on, which will help with uncovering the blockages and releasing them. Even the action of giving it a shape and form will be healing in itself. Being aware of the problem is usually the hardest work.

The main way to give a problem its own identity is to think about where it is located in the body and what it looks and feels like.

Ask the client to think about the problem, thought, or issue that they want healed. They don't have to give you details about what the problem is; they simply need to think about it.

They can close their eyes and think deeply about the problem as well as the potential cause. Ask the client where this issue is in their body and if they can feel it. Do they have a sense of where it is or a likely place it would be? For example, when one feels sad after a breakup, a feeling of heaviness often sits in the heart or chest area. The client may feel tension or pain where the blockage is. If they have no idea, reassure them that there is no wrong answer, and they can simply guess. It's just a starting point.

The next step is to focus on the area and the issue and to try and see what form or shape it has. Ask the client to imagine the problem and try to detect its shape, color, texture, and size. The more detail they can offer, the better. Negative energy often has a distinct feeling to it— it may be heavy, rough, or dark, for instance.

The issue now has a non-verbal, visual identity. You and the client are consciously aware of it, and it can be used as a focal point during Reiki treatment sessions. The client can focus on the image or visualization of this problem being pulled out and sent away as you perform the Reiki treatment.

Performing the Psychic Surgery

1. The client may be lying on a therapy table or seated on a comfortable chair. Draw the power symbol on the palms of both your hands and activate it by saying the name of the symbol three times. You can either clap your hands three times or tap each palm with the index finger of the opposite hand three times.

2. Draw a large power symbol down the front of the client's body and activate it in the manner you have learned. You can also draw a power symbol over each of the client's chakras.

3. Extend your Reiki fingers that will be used in the psychic surgery. You do this by taking hold of your dominant hand's forefinger and thumb with your other hand and imagining that they are the consistency of sticky toffee. Stretch them long in front of you to about 18 inches or so. Inhale deeply as you do this several times. See your fingers growing longer in your mind's eye.

4. Draw and activate the power symbol on each of your extended Reiki fingers and tap them as you say the name of the symbol. Affirm that they are extended and have substance, just as real fingers would.

5. Repeat this process for both hands.

6. Move your hands around, imagining these long, powerful fingers. It's a real Edward Scissorhands moment!

7. Psychic surgery is performed with all of your focus and attention. Use your entire physical, emotional, mental, and spiritual self. Have complete confidence in your

ability, and know that you have the universal power within you to perform this healing act.

8. Set your intention and say a prayer. You're now ready to go ahead.

9. Ask the client to focus on the issue, which now has a very visual identity, and on where it is located in their body. Confirm that they are ready to let it go and be healed.

10. Draw a power symbol over the area.

11. Imagine reaching your extended fingers inside the body of the client and grabbing the negative energy. Pull it out and release it to the ground to rid it of its power.

12. Allow your intuition to guide you with regards to how you pull it out. Sometimes it's a quick and powerful jerk, and other times you pull it out gently and with control. Some energies are big and heavy, while others are light and flexible. Work with what you feel.

13. Breath in as you pull and out as you release. Repeat this motion as many times as you feel is necessary. Keep checking back with the client to determine if the issue has changed size or shape. Ensure they are still okay.

14. Once complete, fill the area with loving light.

15. Step back from the client and make a large karate chop through the air to sever the connection between your body and that of the client.

16. Push your extended fingers back to their normal size while making a blowing sound.

17. If you have the energy and time, and the client is willing, you can follow the psychic surgery with a full Reiki treatment.

It may not be possible to fully remove negative energy or release an entire issue in one session. Elements of the problem may remain, and the client may still have lesions around the emotional wound that need to be dealt with. Sometimes, there is absolutely no change to the shape or size of a problem because the client isn't entirely ready for the blockage to be removed.

One thing that Reiki teaches us is that there is always a higher intelligence at work, and there is a reason for everything. Our growth as spiritual healers is wrapped around this fact.

We can't heal everything and everyone.

We are simply a vessel.

Conclusion

I hope you have enjoyed learning about the fascinating healing power of Reiki, its origins, and its many uses.

As you can see, the power of Reiki can be near infinite. It can be used on yourself, on others that are physically present, on animals, and even on people on the other side of the world. This powerful healing energy has transformed the lives of many around the world and continues to positively impact more and more each day.

We are living during a time where this omnipotent healing energy is more needed than ever. I commend you on taking the time to discover more about it, and wish you the best of luck on your journey with Reiki – whether that involves you becoming a level 3 Reiki master (Shinpiden), or simply booking your first session with a Reiki practitioner!

If you've enjoyed this book, I ask that you please take a couple of minutes to leave me a review on Amazon. I appreciate your honest feedback and support, as it helps me to continue producing quality books tailored to you, my beloved readers, on similar topics that I am passionate about.

I wish you all the best on your journey with Reiki,

Taylor Turner

References

Bedosky, L. (2020, May 12). Reiki: How this energy healing works and its health benefits | Everyday Health.

https://www.everydayhealth.com/Reiki/

Cho Ku Rei. (n.d.). Retrieved from Wikimedia. https://commons.wikimedia.org/wiki/File:Chokurei.jpg

Dai Ko Myo. (n.d.). Retrieved from Wikimedia. https://commons.wikimedia.org/wiki/File:Daikomyo.jpg

Endocrine System. (n.d.). Retrieved from Wikimedia. https://commons.wikimedia.org/wiki/File:1801_The_Endocrine_System.jpg

Griff, A. M. (2017, September 6). Reiki: What is it and are there benefits? Medical News Today. https://www.medicalnewstoday.com/articles/308772#becoming-a-Reiki-practitioner

Hon Sha Ze Sho Nen. (n.d.). Retrieved from Wikimedia. https://commons.wikimedia.org/wiki/File:Honshazeshonen.jpg

IARP. (2014, April 20). What is Reiki? IARP. https://iarp.org/what-is-Reiki/

Lymphatic System. (n.d.). Retrieved from Wikimedia. https://commons.wikimedia.org/wiki/File:Blausen_0623_LymphaticSystem_Female.png

Main Organs. (n.d.). Retrieved from Wikimedia.
https://commons.wikimedia.org/wiki/File:Internal_org
ans.png

Malone, G., & Malone, A. (1998). The essence of Reiki : the Vsui
method of natural healing : a complete guide to 1st &
2nd degree. Transformational Seminars.

Reiki Administrator. (2014, October 15). What is Reiki? Reiki.
https://www.Reiki.org/faqs/what-Reiki

Sei He Ki. (n.d.). Retrieved from Wikimedia.
https://commons.wikimedia.org/wiki/File:SeiHe_Ki_.j
pg

Vlad. (2019, November 12). Hon Sha Ze Sho Nen - The Reiki
symbol for distance healing. Reiki Scoop.
https://Reikiscoop.com/hon-sha-ze-sho-nen-the-Reiki-
symbol-for-distance-healing/